Listen

By Dianne Mohan

Heritage Books Canada

Mohan, Dianne Louise
Listen... a disabled person's plea for your attention
Summary: In part an account of personal experience, *Listen* is also a call for new approaches to ensuring a better quality of life for those with physical or developmental limitations.
First published: Edmonton, Alberta, Canada : Heritage Books Canada, 2007
World-wide Distribution: Trafford Publishing, Victoria, B.C., Canada
I. Mohan, Dianne Louise, 1949 adult, educational, non-fiction
Printed in Canada

U.S. Publisher Cataloging-in-Publication Data (Library of Congress Standards)

Mohan, Dianne Louise
Listen... a disabled person's plea for your attention
Originally first published by Heritage Books Canada, Edmonton, Alberta, 2007

Order this book online at www.trafford.com/07-1165
or email orders@trafford.com

Note for Librarians: A cataloguing record for this book is available from Library and Archives Canada at www.collectionscanada.ca/amicus/index-e.html

Printed in Victoria, BC, Canada.

ISBN: 978-1-4251-3168-5

www.trafford.com

North America & international
toll-free: 1 888 232 4444 (USA & Canada)
phone: 250 383 6864 ♦ fax: 250 383 6804 ♦ email: info@trafford.com

The United Kingdom & Europe
phone: +44 (0)1865 722 113 ♦ local rate: 0845 230 9601
facsimile: +44 (0)1865 722 868 ♦ email: info.uk@trafford.com

10 9 8 7 6 5 4 3 2

Heritage Books Canada acknowledges with thanks the various organizations and societies that support work of this author and our publishing program.

Design by: Max Lietz
Cover Image and Design: Photosbyrubens and Maxwell Design Concepts
Text photo images: Dianne Mohan
Book Developer: Reuben Bauer

PREFACE

"We're disabled, not disposable!" This is the message delivered by author Dianne Mohan in this brief but powerful exploration of what she sees as society's outmoded, often dismissive, attitudes toward so-called "persons of disability."

Approaching a serious subject with both candour and humour, she points to the fact that much of society, through apathy or misunderstanding, continues to buy into hurtful myths about those who are visibly disabled. As a result, the intelligence, talent, and willingness of tens of thousands of Canadians are lost behind the disability label.

Herself affected by a brain tumour and successive seizures which have limited her sight, speech, hearing and mobility, Dianne speaks with authority about a world in which those with physical or developmental limitations tend to experience a loss of dignity and sense of self-worth. In a society that prides itself on its spirit of inclusion, she asks, why should disabled persons continue to face enormous barriers in the community?

The author offers suggestions to help educators, policy makers, the helping professions and the community in general recognize an often overlooked human resource. Even modest changes in attitudes, policies and opportunities, she contends, would help disabled Canadians move out of the shadows to become productive, contributing members of mainstream society.

ACKNOWLEDGMENTS

I am sincerely grateful to the many friends and family members who have helped me over the years. Without their support and encouragement, this book would not have been produced.

In particular, I want to thank Rae Douglas, friend and health care professional, who, from the outset, demonstrated her faith in this project.

Finally, my sincere appreciation to the management and staff of Chateau Sturgeon in Legal, Alberta, whose care and consideration have added so much to the quality of my "second life."

A special thank-you

Many thanks are due to Lois Bridges who agreed to act as my fingers on the keys, enabling me to commit my thoughts and ideas to paper. Her unflagging patience and support inspired me to carry this project through to completion.

This book was written by Dianne Mohan. Because her disability prevented her from physically typing the manuscript, I agreed to handle this task for her.

During several meetings over the course of two years, Dianne communicated the messages she wished to include in her story and these comments, recollections and opinions have been recorded, to the greatest possible degree, in her own words and phrases.

Lois Bridges

ABOUT THE AUTHOR

Dianne Mohan, a native of Saskatchewan who has spent much of her adult life in Alberta, lived her "first life" as a so-called normal person. Diagnosed with an inoperable brain tumour at age 29, this active business woman, co-owner and operator of two Red Deer restaurants, mother of four and energetic contributor to society, would find herself over the next three decades moving gradually into her "second life" – the world of the visibly disabled.

Beyond the obvious challenges of learning to cope with her loss of mobility and communication skills (her ability to think and her sense of humour remain fully intact), Dianne faced her greatest shock when she began to sense that much of society still views persons of disability as "disabled" fist and "persons" second. Pointing to the fact that millions of potentially productive Canadians have been sidelined by physical or developmental limitations, she calls on government policy makers and the general public to rethink attitudes toward the disabled in order to benefit from what she sees as largely untapped resource for society.

Dianne currently resides in a seniors' complex in Legal, Alberta, where she remains in close contact with a large and supportive family, including her four adult children who live nearby.

(L-R) Dianne Mohan, author; and Melanie Mason, daughter and business manager.

TERMINOLOGY

Words Shape Attitudes

Governments, associations of disabled persons, advocacy groups and assorted etiquette gurus have all issued lists of appropriate words and phrases to help society avoid the use of inaccurate, often demeaning, terms to describe persons with disabilities.

For example, we're all accustomed to hearing the word handicapped to describe someone with a disability. (I've used the term myself in this book.) However, it's important to note a handicap and a disability are not the same thing. As the Status of Disabled Persons Secretariat in Ottawa points out, "a **disability** is a functional limitation or restriction of an individual's ability to perform an activity. A **handicap** is an environmental or attitudinal barrier that limits the opportunity for a person to participate fully." For a person with a disability, the handicap could be lack of access to a particular building.

Words to watch:

- Instead of "the disabled," "the handicapped," or "the physically challenged," use "persons with disabilities."
- Instead of saying a person is "wheelchair bound" or "confined to a wheelchair," say he or she "uses a wheelchair." Wheelchairs give us mobility. They don't restrict us.
- Instead of "the blind," refer to "people who are blind, partially sighted or visually impaired."
- Instead of "the deaf," refer to "people who are deaf or hearing impaired."

- Avoid using negative terms such as "afflicted with" or "suffering from." (We rarely see ourselves as afflicted or suffering!)
- Forget such degrading words as "cripple" or "crippled," "abnormal" or "subnormal." Say instead "he or she has a disability."
- Instead of the term "epileptic," refer to "a person with epilepsy."
- Avoid words such as "fit," "attack" or "spell." Instead, say "seizure."
- Instead of "invalid," say "person with a disability."
- Avoid derogatory terms such as "mental patient," "mentally diseased," or "mentally challenged," say "person with a disability."
- Avoid the term "victim." Persons with disabilities rarely see themselves as victims.

Common Stereotypes to Avoid:

- Disability is a huge tragedy.
- A person with a disability is an object of pity and charity.
- Those with disabilities don't care to participate in society and don't have plans, aspirations or a need to achieve personal goals.
- Persons with disabilities want to be considered "special."

Tips on Etiquette

- Avoid standing and talking for long periods to someone in a wheelchair. Find a chair and sit down to talk.

- Speak directly to the person with the disability, not to his or her companion or assistant.
- Ensure that a person who is deaf or hearing impaired has a clear view of your face during conversation.
- Don't raise your voice as if talking to a child. Speak in your normal fashion.
- Don't interrupt a person with a speech impairment in order to "help out" by finishing sentences. Listen patiently, then ask for clarification if necessary.
- Don't worry about using phrases such a "go for a walk" when addressing someone in a wheelchair; or "see you later" when talking to a person who is blind or visually impaired.
- Remember that the majority of persons with disabilities are typical of society in general. They expect and deserve to be included in the community and don't look for special treatment.

TABLE OF CONTENTS

INTRODUCTION

Since my life has been split almost evenly between the world of the so-called normal and the world of the disabled, I can say with some authority that normal is definitely better. If my first life was relatively smooth and predictable, my second life has been anything but. Still, it's *my* life and I'm convinced it's up to me to live it to the fullest extent.

I didn't recognize it at the time but today I know that in 1979, when I was diagnosed with an inoperable brain tumour, my second life had begun. At age 29, I was about to join a new crowd. Before too long, I'd be known primarily not as wife, mother, homemaker, business woman and contributing member of society but rather as "a person with a disability."

My purpose in writing this book is to remind readers — including longtime and newly disabled folks and those who care for them — that as disabled persons, we *can* learn to play the cards we're dealt without losing our sense of dignity and self-worth. It's a double-barreled educational challenge. First, it involves learning to value ourselves; and, second, it means helping others learn to value us for what we can contribute to society.

According to Statistics Canada, more than 4.3 million Canadians, including roughly half a million Albertans, are classified as disabled. These are startling numbers, representing a substantial force in society. How sad it is to think that in far too many cases, the warmth, the talent, the expertise, the humour, the willingness of so many people are all somehow lost behind that discouraging word "disabled."

It's a harsh comparison, but I can't help wondering if there aren't some similarities to the Holocaust. Clearly the millions of disabled persons in Canada are not being deliberately tortured or killed. Still, there is no doubt that thousands have lost what should have been their rightful place in the community. And, as in the era of wartime atrocities, society at large is seemingly unaware of this sad and unnecessary loss to the world. I'm convinced that ignorance, apathy, and the many distractions of modern life are all part of this picture. Despite international declarations, countless studies and well-intentioned government strategies, the potential of a huge part of the nation's population is simply overlooked. We deserve more. Society deserves more.

Because my journey into disability has been a gradual exercise, I've had the relative luxury of adapting slowly to the changes taking place in my life. I realize that those whose disability results from a sudden traumatic incident or those who were born disabled have had no such luxury. If my own experience has given me anything in the way of a unique perspective it is in the realization that we don't have to be lost to society. We can contribute. Even minor changes in attitude, in services and in opportunities for the disabled can make a huge difference. And in some small way, I'm hopeful this book will play a part in the process.

Dianne Mohan

Chapter - 1

WHERE'S DIANNE?

Where is Dianne? Dianne is with her seven siblings in this picture. You will find her in the back row, third from the right in a checkered dress.

In 1979, I underwent the first of a series of operations that I believed would solve the problem — mainly fierce headaches that had plagued me since adolescence and which seemed to get worse with each year. That first operation produced a chilling diagnosis: "inoperable" brain tumour. Not that that meant I would die right away. Nor would it stop the operations. Seven or eight operations later, however, the diagnosis remains unchanged. Apparently my very own 'astrocytoma of the cerebellum' is here to stay.

What followed that first operation was a kind of honeymoon phase. I felt relatively healthy; I was soon back at work, running two businesses, caring for husband and family. Much of my old energy returned and I was optimistic the worst was over.

It wasn't.

Perhaps I was naive to think I could simply go back to my old life. Maybe I felt my legendary pig-headedness and something my friends called "spunk" were enough to keep me well. Within a few years I would learn otherwise as I found myself taking my first, wobbly steps into a whole new world. As I progressed from cane to walker to wheelchair, I was soon to meet another challenge. A stroke would introduce me to a world that seemed slightly off balance. Over the years, it has robbed my body of coordination, left me deaf, seeing double and forced to wear an eyepatch, and produced the kind of garbled speech that tends to draw blank stares.

No matter how hard I tried to ignore the truth, I finally had to accept the fact that I had become unemployable, a person who seemed to need help at every turn. My once hopeful future looked increasingly bleak and I had to learn to bite my tongue to keep from railing at the injustice of it all It took a long time to dawn on me that virtually everything in my life had changed. It wasn't until years later that I realized what had happened. With that first operation, I had truly begun my second life.

In the years between 1979 and the present I've experienced a whole new phase in my education, learning what others, disabled from birth, must know instinctively. We're "different." This is even acknowledged in the Human Rights Declaration, which has separate provisions for handicapped people. Even so, I'm convinced that different means neither better nor worse. I now know that the disabled (the politically savvy call us "people with disabilities" while the less politically correct call us "the handicapped," "the physically or mentally challenged," or, heaven forbid, "cripples") are not an amorphous blob. We can't be lumped together any more than seniors or racecar drivers or policemen can be seen as all alike. We're who we are — individuals with our own personalities, our own strengths and weaknesses, our own dreams and goals for the future.

I've also come to another realization. No matter what society sees in me — with my wheelchair, my eyepatch, my hearing aid, my scrambled speech — I am still me. Miraculously, my brain has remained healthy. Those who can see beyond the awkward movements, the pirate patch and the funny talk see that I am still Dianne.

Chapter - 2

MY FIRST LIFE

Dianne with her parents on her wedding day in 1969.

If you can't stand the cold, you'd better arrange not to be born and brought up in Saskatchewan. Unfortunately nobody gave me this bit of advice. So when I look back now on what was obviously a very happy childhood in the small southeastern Saskatchewan community of Plato, some of my clearest memories are of shivering through winters and delighting in long, warm summers full of picnics, berry picking, area sports days, visits to the "home farm" and whatever mischief happened to spring to mind. It was all homemade fun and it kept me and my siblings engrossed in what I realize now was a safe, family-oriented world. Clearly my "first life" was normal in every way.

As the oldest of eight children, I soon adopted a take-charge attitude. Always stubborn and competitive, I had to be the best. I'm not saying I *was* the best but that was always my goal. In school, I desperately strove to be head of the class and sometimes succeeded. The competitive drive also contributed to my love of sports. Volley ball, basketball, baseball — you name it, I played it. In fact our whole family played baseball and when my dad got too old to play, he coached. I recall us going to sports days every weekend for three to four months during the summer. And if we kids were routinely edged away from the concession booths (too expensive!), our ever-prudent mom would come armed with a big cooler full of sandwiches.

If I had to think of a single word to describe the world of my childhood, it would be "closeknit." Our ever-expanding family worked and played together. And, although nobody used words like morals and values, our parents somehow made sure we had a good grounding in both. There was always something to do and someone to do it with. And, as I was to realize later, there were other benefits to being part of a big family, not the least of which were lots of family support and the fact that there was always somebody to argue with.

Beyond family, Plato was a community where everyone knew everyone else. In fact, I've often said that since my grandparents were original settlers in the province, I'm more than likely related to half the people in Saskatchewan. Although we lived in town, our links to the farming community were strong since the family farm was located only about six miles outside Plato.

Visits to the farm were a delight and fertile ground for a bunch of young mischief-makers. One of our more memorable capers involved getting up in my uncle's hayloft, where my cousin and I discovered that by swinging long boards in the air, we could drive the resident pigeons to exhaustion. Once they dropped from the rafters, we could even pick them up. I had always assumed pigeons were white. But I soon discovered they came in a variety of colours from grey to mauve to purple. That was when we decided to add to uncle's "herd" of pigeons. Off we went to an abandoned farm about a mile and a half away, determined to find pigeons with the most exotic plumage around. As we had hoped, there were pigeons in the barn. The board swinging began in earnest and soon we had some vividly coloured birds for our own barn. Unfortunately, the first person we met coming home was my uncle. It wasn't a good scene. Now if somebody asked me to hang on to a dirty old pigeon, I'd think they were nuts.

Another scheme that seemed truly brilliant at the time involved creating an underground mice-rearing facility, with the help of some big jars my aunt used for canning. We thought it was ingenious. My uncle, however, thought otherwise. We simply couldn't understand why adults didn't see the possibilities of such a scheme.

When we got a bit older, our youthful exuberance was channeled into even more daring adventures. Prime among them was tipping over outhouses — a nerve jangling exercise that we somehow found hilarious. Unless you happened to be the biffy owner — or worse still, the occupant — this was generally considered by the community to be a dumb but harmless rite of passage for local youngsters. Without the distractions of shopping malls, video games and the like, we were left to our own devices when it came to entertainment.

During the winter, my siblings and I would become curling orphans as our parents competed in every bonspiel within a 50-miles radius of home. They were very good curlers and generally won. While I always felt the cold, they never seemed to notice the weather although I imagine the rinks in those days were not all that warm. I used to say I must have been switched with another baby at birth because I certainly didn't inherit my parents' indifference to frigid temperatures. Years later, when I reluctantly agreed to my family getting snowmobiles, I would get so bundled up against the cold that they'd have to roll me out the door.

In our opinion as kids, Plato had a lot going for it, including a school that went as far as Grade 8. After that, we'd head for Eston, 15 miles away where the school offered Grades 9 to 12. There were also occasional family visits to Rosetown, the closest thing to a city we were likely to encounter growing up. After highschool, the next step for many of us would be to set our sights on Saskatoon some 135 miles northwest. When I made that journey, it was with the idea firmly in mind that I'd work for a year before enrolling in university. I didn't realize at the time that my life would take a slightly different twist.

I'm sure life as a child in Plato wasn't perfect. Nothing is. In fact, I had already had a glimpse of the "real-world" concerns that would one day dominate my life. I knew people in our community who were severely handicapped; and there was a stint in my teen years as a counselor with Camp Easter Seal at Saskatchewan's Lake Manitou, where the focus was on people with physical or mental problems. I suspect it never occurred to me that I might one day be in a similar position. After all, I was young, healthy and about to take on the world. In fact, except for the occasional headache, I can recall few blemishes on that pleasant, safe, supportive world in which I grew up. Surely, adulthood would be equally satisfying and uneventful.

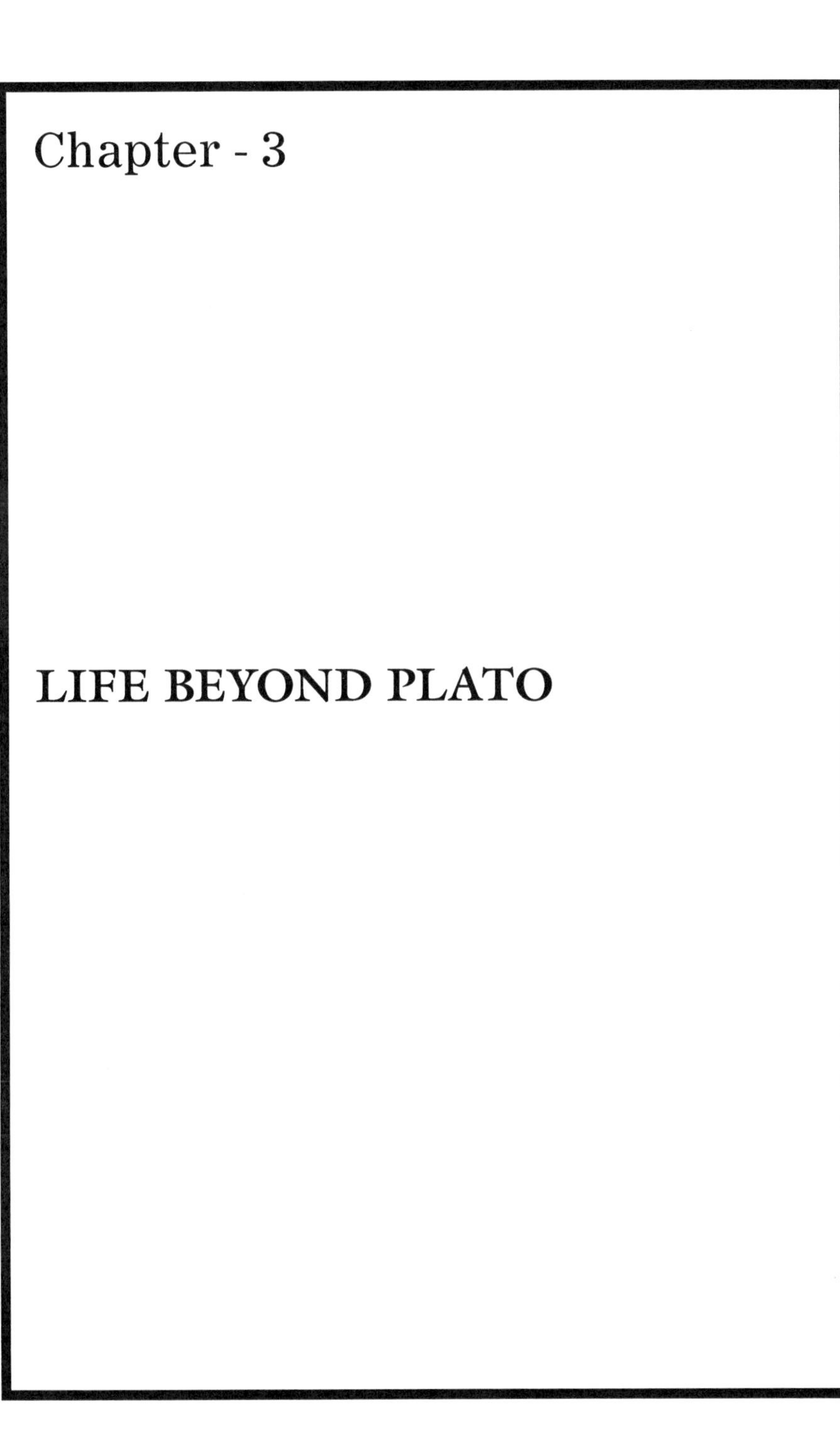

Chapter - 3

LIFE BEYOND PLATO

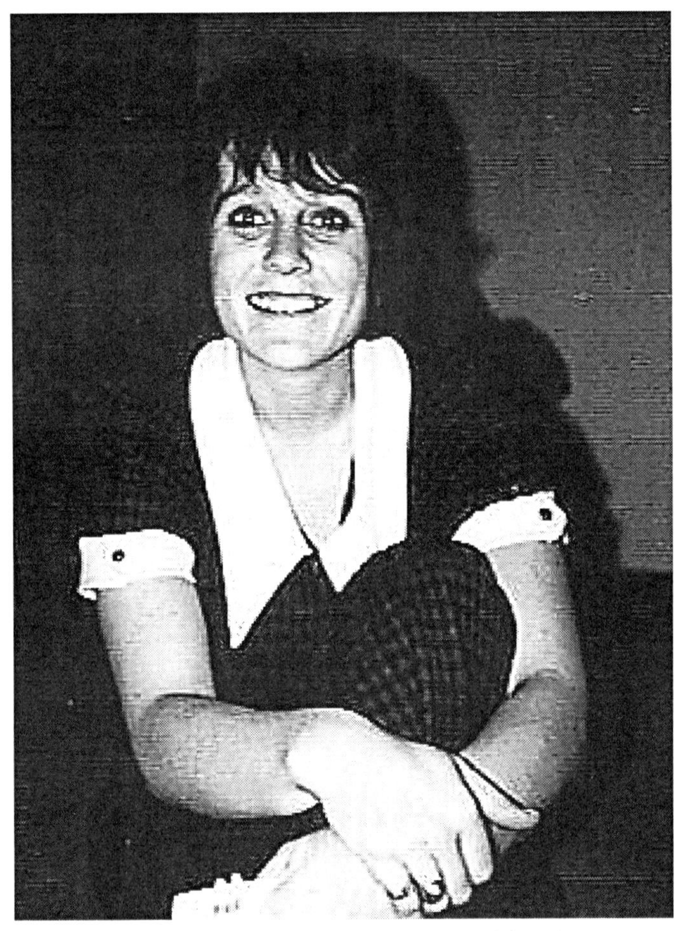

Dianne, young and healthy, in 1974 before her operation.

After I graduated from highschool in 1969, I moved to Saskatoon and a job with A&W as hostess/coordinator and counselor for the company's three Saskatoon outlets. My duties included counseling, training and retraining staff. It was a great job and I loved it. By the time I was named assistant manager for A&W in Saskatoon, I knew I was hooked on the restaurant business. At that point I had a new career in mind and all my plans for university went down the drain.

Soon I was married and starting a family — a son and a daughter, now both in their thirties. It seemed like I had truly become an adult but, as I now realize, both my husband and I were far too immature to make our marriage work. Our divorce was remarkably civil, however, and with little or no animosity involved. We simply moved on.

Soon after my divorce, I moved to Red Deer with the children, remarried and, with my new husband, launched a restaurant business in that city. There were two sides to the business — a pizza and steak restaurant and a fine dining establishment, both served by a central kitchen Since our family continued to grow with the addition of two sons, life in those years was busy, often hectic. But I had always had lots of energy so if something needed doing, I did it. Now when I think of coping with the management of two businesses, a home, a husband and four children all at the same time, it blows my mind. But at the time, I simply didn't think about it.

Life in general was good — with one exception. The headaches I'd had since I was 15 were getting progressively worse. At first, they came only now and then and all it seemed to take was an aspirin or two to dull the pain. In fact, it took almost 15 years for them to get bad enough to be of serious concern. By my late twenties they were becoming more frequent and more intense. At first doctors thought they were migraine headaches. But finally the pain became so severe I ended up in hospital in Red Deer, undergoing every test known to God and man. Red Deer doctors couldn't find the cause, however, so they sent me by ambulance to the University of Alberta Hospital in Edmonton, where I underwent the first of a series of operations on my head.

After the first operation, I remember the doctor telling me all about it in doctor talk. I asked if he would mind explaining it in English. Luckily he had a good sense of humour and didn't take offence at my comment. He said I had a valve like the valve on a pressure cooker behind my right ear. It was growing shut and that's what was causing the headaches. After 15 years of getting progressively worse, the valve was now completely shut, causing my brain to fill up with fluid. Doctors put in a shunt on the right side of my head that drains fluid to my stomach. Later, they decided one of these wasn't enough so they put another in on the left side. These were replaced over the years as new technology was developed; and that, of course, meant more operations.

That wasn't the whole story. I learned that an inoperable cancerous brain tumour was at the heart of my problems. I was told there were two kinds — one type that grows up the spine and another that develops behind the fourth ventricle of the brain. I had the second type, a tumour so well hidden that doctors couldn't even get a piece big enough for a proper diagnosis. This meant no one could give me a definite answer about what to expect in future. At the time, doctors were aware of only about 200 similar cases, although I'm told the condition is not considered that rare any more.

After the operation I had radiation treatments which left me bald as a cue ball for almost a year before my hair grew back. That meant wearing a wig or one of the many turbans I collected. I recall having one in every colour imaginable.

There was also chemotherapy. I was given pills and I recall the doctor saying I might gain a bit of weight. In no time flat I was in maternity clothes. My eyes looked like two burnt holes in the snow. I had always had a medium build but I absolutely ballooned and, as my husband liked to point out at the time, I looked like the Goodyear Blimp. I gained 50 pounds and was absolutely devastated. I'd put my blue jeans in the wash and by the time they came out, they'd no longer fit. That's how quick it was. It was unbelievable and I spent a lot of time sitting at home and crying over my appearance. I didn't want anybody to see me. Once I quit the pills, however, that weight came right off. I forget now how long I took them.

Despite the news about the tumour and the unsettling aftereffects, I came out of that first surgery feeling relatively okay and would stay that way for the next seven or eight years. I was like a leukemia patient, experiencing remissions. Between them, my condition was gradually deteriorating but it was never clear how far down I would go. I remember the doctors telling me the head is the last frontier in medicine and they don't have all the answers.

In the meantime, I regained some energy and was soon back at work. I sincerely believed that now that the blood and guts were behind me, everything would go back to normal. I did make one concession to my new reality. I had always worn two-inch heels to work. Now I wore flats, which meant I didn't feel quite so tottery on my feet. It was no big deal. At that point I didn't look funny and a stranger would never have guessed my condition. Later, I would be accused a couple of times of being drunk because of my awkward gait. But at this point I was still able to manage quite well with lower heels.

Despite my optimism about the future (I was determined to beat whatever it was that threatened my health and my so-called normal life), after a half dozen years I had to face the fact that everything in my world was slowly but surely changing.

Chapter - 4

THE JOURNEY BEGINS

During the restaurant years, with her eldest son, just before her first operation.

After my first operation at the University of Alberta Hospital, the focus of my life became the Royal Alexandra Hospital in Edmonton. Every time I turned around I had to go to the hospital for some procedure or other. Over the years my head would be opened up for examination or repair another six or seven times. It was after about the fourth stay there that I began to notice something strange. Each time I showed up, staff would take my medical history. Wouldn't it have been simpler to take a photocopy of my medical records and save us both time? I was certainly there often enough. In fact I was such a familiar sight, somebody once asked me, "Didn't you used to be a doctor here?"

Still, in those early years after the first operation, life went on more or less as usual. My husband and I continued to operate two Red Deer restaurants: Venice House and Noah's. He was a terrific public relations person and it was definitely his personality that helped build the business. Later we would sell it for reasons that had nothing to do with my illness. And later still, our marriage would dissolve. There's an old saying that when the going gets tough, the tough get going — and that's just what my ex did. He left. You never know what another person is thinking.

At this stage, however, I was still well enough to work. In the mid-1980s I was self-employed as general assistant to senior citizens of the Meadowcroft Apartment Seniors Housing complex in Edmonton. My parents were caretakers of this complex which had 16 floors with 30 apartments per floor. I worked for some of the residents, cleaning, washing drapes and so on. I know now that my body was failing a little at a time during this period but I could still do this kind of work. And even then there was always the hope that I'd recover.

In fact, I was lucky to have work. After we sold the business, I filled out applications for dozens of jobs but was told more times than enough that I was overqualified. I could have screamed. I suspected it was because employers focused on my cane and the patch I had to wear over my eye after the first operation. My speech was slightly impaired by then (it would get worse after the stroke) and I guess that, unless they were blind and deaf, prospective employers got the hint I was disabled. I never did get a job again, although my brain was not affected. I couldn't understand it. Here I was with smarts enough to do all sorts of things — everything from making schedules to counseling employees — but all of a sudden I couldn't even get a job cleaning washrooms. I was beginning to get a sense of what my second life might be like.

At one point I was sent to a psychoanalyst for testing. He concluded that I had superior intelligence which was nice to know — but not so great when you can't find even the most menial job.

On the home front things were better. To my kids, all of whom were still at home after my first operation, I was still Mom. I had always been independent and so my health problems didn't seem like a huge deal to any of us. If I had a problem it was with siblings and parents who tended to become overprotective. I know they don't want to see me struggle but I've learned that you have to find a different way to handle tasks that have become difficult. Rather than helping or encouraging me to do things in different ways, they frequently ended up doing the job for me. I know they were acting out of love and concern but I had to try to salvage as much of my independence as possible.

Although I haven't had an operation for the past decade or more (and if another operation is suggested I plan to refuse), I have had a few scary moments. After one of these operations I was in a coma for 40 days. My mother was told to call all my family in because they didn't expect me to pull through. Although I was out of it for weeks, I did remember bits and pieces: doctors and nurses, family members and friends drifting in and out of view. It seemed like all of this took place in about a day. I don't know where I was for the other 39 days.

Then there was the incident of the leaking brain fluid. There was no pain but I remember feeling a dampness on the back of my neck as if I had just shampooed my hair and it was dampening my collar. The fluid was seeping right through my skin. The doctor wanted me to come in for an operation but, having had my head sliced up six or seven times already, I decided to pass this time around. I reasoned that, although we have two of everything else, we just have one head and I'd kind of like to keep it intact. As it turned out, the problem just cleared up on its own.

After the brain operations I had physical therapy but I suspect it was a disappointment to the therapists as well as myself. They were hoping to be able to teach me how to walk again. I think by the time they finished I could walk about seven steps but it was pretty tough to do anything about my balance. Apparently one's sense of balance is located in the fourth ventricle of the brain and in the ears — in my case, a double whammy as I was no great shakes in either department.

After the first operations, I was pretty wobbly but I was learning to compensate. Later, after the stroke, my balance was badly affected. On more than one occasion I've wakened up to find myself kissing the carpet or the pavement. Although I've never been seriously injured by these nose-dives, it's an unnerving experience for those who come to my rescue. And since one particularly severe seizure in 2004 that left me face down on the ground beside my wheelchair, I've been forced to forego many of the outings that I once enjoyed. It's been decided I can't go out unless there's somebody with me, which essentially means I don't go out much. No big sacrifice for me in winter, I admit — but I certainly hope to have my wheelchair in gear again next summer.

Some years ago, when I had the first stroke, I recall my hands and feet feeling funny. I must be dumber than a sack of moose horns because it wasn't until somebody suggested I might have had a stroke, that I realized what had happened. Years later, the ends of my fingers are still tingly. If I want to pick something up I have to think about it. The pinch part of my fingers, whatever that's called, doesn't work properly. In any case, between the tumour and the stroke, I'm a mess. I can't write, I talk funny and I see double. The more tired I get, the bigger the problem with my eye. It doesn't matter which eye —one of them has to close. Otherwise I'm seeing double and everything's on a tilt.

It's a little tougher to gauge what effect the stroke had on my mobility. I couldn't walk before so I'm not sure if the stroke added to that problem.

The speech problem is something else again. Before I had the stroke, you could hardly make me stop talking. My mom used to say if I'd just keep my mouth shut, nobody would know I'm disabled. Strangely, I don't notice how funny I sound. The words are in my head and I think I'm saying what's in my head. It's like listening to your voice on a tape recorder. You always think: that's not me! I've heard myself talk on tape and it's quite horrifying so I know that at least half the people I talk to have no idea what I'm saying.

In short, my communication skills went to hell in a handbasket after my stroke. At one time, for example, people admired my handwriting. It was very good. Now I write worse than a doctor and that's pretty bad. I could write a grocery list today and two days later I won't know what I wrote.

For several years I was able to continue "my second life" on my own in Lloydminster — a location that placed me roughly half way between my three sons in Edmonton and my daughter in Saskatoon. Eventually, however, the children began worrying about me living alone and the search was on for a new housing arrangement. The best choice was a seniors home operated by the Sturgeon Foundation in Legal, Alberta. The rooms are pleasant; the company is good; the meals are excellent and there's generally someone around to share a game of cards. Although there's no nursing care, there's a call button in the bathroom in case of emergencies.

When I first moved in, I was able to handle things like bathing on my own. I remember declaring to anyone who would listen that the day someone else had to bathe me would be the day I would run away from home. So much for that bit of cockiness! I'm now extremely thankful for the assistance I get with bathing and other tasks. Just being clean and presentable far outweighs any humiliation I might have felt at first.

Chapter - 5

OBSERVATIONS OF A SECOND-LIFER

With daughter Melanie in 1980 shortly after Dianne's first operation.

Since joining the ranks of the disabled. I've found myself pondering issues that I gave little if any thought to in my so-called normal life. I've discovered what is essentially a lost society — hundreds of people sitting at home, taking up space, doing nothing, simply because of the way they look or the way they talk. Every community has this underutilized resource and it's such a waste.

I've noticed as well society's tendency to lump all disabled people together. In fact, we're just plain ordinary people — some good, some bad; some likable, some twits, some with a positive outlook on life and some who appear to despise everyone and everything around them. As a result, I've learned there is no special *rule* for dealing with disabled persons. I suggest the safest bet is to stick to the same rules of decency and civility that apply to relationships with society in general. Behind the disability, we're all simply people. And if it takes some extra time, sympathy and understanding to ensure that the disabled become contributing members of society, surely it's worthwhile making such an effort.

I'm convinced that changing attitudes on both sides would make a huge difference in the lives of both disabled persons and mainstream society. If, for example, those with physical or mental impairments were treated like persons first and foremost, their feelings of inadequacy and worthlessness would surely diminish. We would be far more likely to value ourselves. Sadly, however, far too many disabled folks are simply warehoused. Often it's because the family is embarrassed to have them around. With time and patience could many of these folks not be trained to do the jobs the non-disabled tend to avoid? Not too many so-called normal folks aspire to cleaning washrooms or handling routine tasks they consider boring or beneath their attention. Many disabled folks would jump at a chance for such a job. It could be a first step in learning to value oneself, losing the feeling of total inadequacy. On a positive note, I've heard recently of a government-sponsored employment agency dealing solely with disabled workers. Let's hope this becomes the norm everywhere.

I'm not suggesting everyone with a disability, particularly a visible disability, has given up. People of exceptional talent and determination have overcome enormous physical challenges to make lasting contributions to society. The names of Terry Fox and Rick Hansen spring to mind. Both overcame serious disabilities to have an enormous positive impact on society at home and abroad. Internationally renowned physicist Stephen Hawking has overcome incredible physical challenges to make huge contributions to the world of science. And we've all marveled at the artists who have defied paralysis or lack of motor skills to become mouth painters, producing exceptional works of art.

Behind these success stories, however, there's another very different scenario. Sometimes through lack of family and community support, sometimes because of society's negative attitudes toward the disabled, thousands of Canadians are failing to live up to their potential. For example, I met a woman who told me she had never lived at home until she was in her late teens. Apparently ashamed of their developmentally disabled daughter, her family had shipped her off to an institution where she spent her entire childhood. Another woman confided that, until she was an adult, no one had ever bothered to teach her about money. As a child, if she was sent to the store to buy a quart of milk, she wasn't likely to come back with any change if she happened to encounter an unprincipled clerk. She simply didn't know the difference and no one considered she was worth teaching or capable of learning. Both perceptions proved to be wrong.

In far too many cases, this loss to society is both unfortunate and unnecessary. The difference between being considered an asset and being seen as a liability to society may not be that great. Early assessment of aptitudes among the developmentally and physically impaired, along with a greater effort to encourage, teach and employ them, could dramatically change this picture. Volunteer organizations are always on the lookout for people. Boards and agencies could benefit from the advice and experience of members who are disabled. Someone could well handle dozens of office tasks in a wheelchair; and the possibilities for disabled folks who are computer literate should be virtually endless.

I'm convinced that a bit more education, a bit more understanding on the part of both the disabled and mainstream society would see many of us become contributors rather than simply a problem to be dealt with. Every disabled person I've spoken to has similar comments: "We have no desire to be leeches; we'd much rather be productive."

For what they're worth, here are a few more observations from the wheelchair:

First impressions

In a recent newspaper article, a spokesperson for the Parkinson's Society noted that people often equate slow movement and slow speech with a slow mind. How true! If we're physically handicapped and it shows, surely we must be a tad lacking in the brain department as well. For example, when people see me coming with a patch on my eye, in a wheelchair and talking funny, it's not likely to occur to them that I actually have a brain, that I might be able to accomplish all sorts of things. It appears to me that the majority of people — and of course I'm not including everyone — tend to generalize about the disabled. And, sad to say, their view of us more often than not is negative.

I recently read the account of a woman — an athlete and runner who had been hit by a cyclist riding down the sidewalk. She suffered a brain injury from which she has been gradually recovering. She, too, has noted the change in attitude of the people she comes in contact with. Like many of us, she's discovered that a disability — particularly if it involves the brain — tends to make others think of you as stupid. According to the news report, this lady noticed that sometimes she doesn't get the respect she deserves. And, like many of us with brain-related or other disabilities, she is having to learn to tolerate ignorance. Again, public education about the disabled appears to hold the answer.

I know of so many otherwise kind, well meaning people who could still do with a few pointers in dealing with disabled folks. There's no doubt in anyone's mind, for example, that I'm handicapped. And since it's so easy to make assumptions based on appearance, I suspect that I and others like me are sometimes pigeonholed as weird or stupid. We often suspect what normal folks think of us. We would hope they care as much about what we think of them. In my own case, people watching has become one of my favourite pursuits and I've often said that if they ever invent a machine that reads thoughts, I'm sunk!

All of us like to be liked and admired by our peers. For social events, it's normal to pay considerable attention to one's hair, makeup and clothing. If a non-disabled person were going to an event involving a group of disabled people, would they take the same care with how they look? I would hope they'd pay us that courtesy — a small sign of respect, perhaps, but very important. The loss of society's respect is one of the toughest pills that many handicapped people have to swallow.

Sometimes the lack of respect is clearly unintentional. It took me a few years to realize this, but I've had to admit recently that I haven't been right about anything in the last quarter century. If I'm in the company of "normal" people and a question arises, someone else's answer is invariably accepted over mine. I may have a bit more trouble getting it out, but you'd think that, based simply on the law of averages, my answer would occasionally have to be the right one.

I've also learned that first impressions can produce one of two results: the kind of offhand or careless treatment that suggests this disabled person won't know the difference; or the overly solicitous treatment that tends to smother and embarrass us. I remember once in a mall food court, having coffee with an acquaintance, I was introduced to a man who I'm sure was about to pat me on the head when he realized how disabled I am. He was clearly embarrassed and uncomfortable and it was obvious he saw only the disability and not the person. It's the kind of condescension that tends to rile disabled folks. And it simply underscores the need to help society in general understand and accept that we are just people. Is it really so tough to look beyond the disability and see us for what we are?

Even when the disability is invisible, we quickly learn to protect ourselves from instant judgments. I once talked to a man who looked as normal as apple pie. He told me he was handicapped — something in his chest that wasn't right. He said, "Nobody at work knows I'm handicapped and that's the way I want it. I just want to go to work and do my job, then go home. I see how visibly disabled people get treated. The only people who know I'm handicapped are my family. At home somebody's always fussing around me, putting my feet up or a cushion behind my back. I don't want that at work."

Hey! I've become invisible!

I suspect everyone in a wheelchair or those with some sort of visible disability have encountered this more than once. At a store, in a restaurant, on the street, glances shift away when you arrive on the scene. And if you're with someone else, questions or remarks are directed to your "normal" companion. In particular, I recall one incident from my restaurant days in Red Deer. A man from Michener Centre (a facility that houses mentally and physically disabled people) came in for lunch with six or seven residents of the centre. The waitress asked the man in charge of the group, "What do they want?" He replied, "Why don't you ask them and find out?" She hadn't meant to offend. She was simply making an assumption based on physical appearance. It's just one more example of the prevailing attitude toward disabled people. People are afraid of the unknown but perhaps, with a bit of education, they might find there's nothing to fear.

I've discovered, as well, that when you're handicapped, conversation tends to go over top of you, around you, but never directly to you. As one non-disabled person discovered, this is frustrating, aggravating and humiliating. When I was living in Lloydminster, a professor at the college asked me to be a guest speaker at a session for students training in the home care field. The students sat in a circle around the room and I was telling them what it was like to be handicapped. I asked for a volunteer and told other class members they could talk to each other but they couldn't talk to the girl who volunteered. Acting as a disabled person, she hopped around the room on her chair. There was plenty of conversation all around her but nobody talked to her. After five minutes I asked her how she liked it. "It stunk," she said. Bingo! Hopefully this exercise helped the class understand that, as caregivers, they should watch out for this kind of situation. Eventually, this lack of engagement takes a toll. I'm no expert, but I've been on both sides of the fence so I know that disabled people often think there's no point in bothering to talk if nobody's going to listen.

After I became disabled, I began to notice that in a crowd, friends and relatives often simply quit talking to me —I suppose for a variety of reasons. I'm sure they weren't being intentionally unkind. Some may have thought talking took too much effort on my part; some are just thoughtless; and some may have figured I had nothing useful to contribute to the conversation. This can lead to other problems. When somebody does speak directly to you or ask a question, you realize you have to answer quickly or the golden moment will pass! Talking with your mouth full breaks a cardinal rule of etiquette, for example. But I suspect many a disabled person has figured it's a rule worth breaking if the conversation turns in your direction. Experience has taught us that if you wait to be polite, the conversation will move away and you'll never get to offer your opinion.

As a longtime chatterbox, I probably find it more frustrating than most to be excluded from the conversation. Sometimes I wish everyone could read the sign I have up on my wall: "Stay tuned. I could say something brilliant at any moment."

I've fallen and I can't get up

For anyone who hasn't spent the last decade in a cave, the "I've fallen and I can't get up" spots on TV spring to mind whenever annoying ads are being discussed. The truth is, disabled persons often do need help and we'd be in a real jam without it. Still, I suspect we've all seen the overreaction of family and friends in the face of even minor incidents. In my own case, I try to remind them that not every dumb, careless, forgetful moment in my life is due to my disability. It's likely I stubbed the odd toe or forgot the odd name during normal years as well.

In fact, I was always dismal at remembering names. Faces, yes. Names, not a hope. Now if I forget someone's name, it's seen as a sure sign that the old grey cells are dwindling due to my condition. Very frustrating!

I recall an incident when I was part of a social gathering at my sister's house. One of the guests, who had gone upstairs to the bathroom, caught her foot on the rug as she was coming back down and took a header down the stairs. As soon as it was clear she wasn't hurt, we all laughed and someone said, "No more wine for you." I remember thinking if it had been me, alarm bells would have gone off and the ambulance would be at the door immediately. Care and concern are wonderful and those of us who have caring families are exceptionally lucky. But just sometimes the cause of our predicament is simply carelessness and not our disabilities.

I once counted 18 bruises between my ankle and knee. I was living on my own in Lloydminster and I knew what I had to do to compensate for my balance problems but, as they say, familiarity breeds contempt. I had simply got careless and had a few falls. Simply put, it was my own fault and a good reminder that I'd have to take better care in future.

I recall another incident. Visiting with a group in a coffee shop, someone knocked over the flower vase. My friend simply picked it up. No big deal! I remember thinking, thank goodness it was you and not me. I suspect that *would* have been a big deal! It's why we try so hard to avoid such incidents. Let me tell you, trying to be perfect can be a bit of a strain.

Some unfortunate incidents are simply the result of being in the wrong place at the wrong time. Once, in Lloydminster I was navigating my wheelchair down the sidewalk when the driver of a half-ton truck wheeled out of the nearby KFC outlet and literally mowed me down. The next thing I remember was waking up surrounded by cops and ambulance personnel ready to whisk me off to the hospital. This event took place on the Saskatchewan side of the border city and when I looked into the legal ramifications of what had happened I was told that Saskatchewan had adopted a "no-fault" insurance system. My lawyer said, "If he'd pushed you another 20 feet you'd have been in Alberta and you'd have had a better chance of being able to sue." He was a good lawyer and, in the end, he at least shamed the insurance company into paying to repair my wheelchair. I also got a new jacket out of it so I suppose it wasn't a total loss.

Don't worry. It's okay to laugh

I think a sense of humour is crucial to people in my situation. I remember once when I lived in Lloydminster, a man delivering Meals on Wheels came to my home. He was new to the program, all dressed up in a suit and tie and obviously a little uncomfortable with his new role. I had been getting ready to move and trying to get everything packed. I was totally exhausted and fed up with the clutter. He surveyed the mess and asked if there was anything more he could do for me. I looked around and said, "A gallon of gasoline and a match would be nice!" Poor fellow. He didn't know what to make of it. I think people are often surprised to find the disabled can laugh and make jokes — often at our own expense. They can't believe that anyone in our predicament could retain a sense of humour. There I am, visibly handicapped — and there's an instant judgment. Surely somebody like me must be totally p'd off with life and certainly not about to make a joke.

On another occasion, when I was using the Handivan service, the driver who regularly helped me to the house and carried my purse teased me about how much it weighed. The next time he came, I had commandeered the wheels off one of the kids' old skateboards and attached them to my purse. It gave him a good laugh. He was someone who had learned that if you treat disabled people as normal, they'll react normally. Well okay, that was a bit weird — but I'm convinced there's a lesson in there somewhere.

Without coaching, kids often get it right

I find children are more outspoken than adults. For example, they'll simply ask what happened to my eye. Parents shush them but I don't mind such questions. In fact, this matter-of-fact acceptance is refreshing. I don't normally volunteer the information but if someone asks, I tell them. Actually, after seeing all the misconceptions people have about disabled persons, a few questions and answers may be just what's needed to destroy some of the myths surrounding disabled folks.

At the other end of the spectrum, people often have an idea in their minds about what a handicapped person is and they tend to pass this concept on to their kids. So the youngster grows up with the same idea as the parents.

On one occasion in Camrose, I was going to the hospital and couldn't find access for my wheelchair. A young boy about nine years old saw me on the road and yelled, "You're supposed to be on the sidewalk." I wasn't in a very good mood so I yelled back, "Go tell your parents to build some damn accesses." Where does a nine year old get the idea he can talk to an adult like that? I suspect just one place — at home. That child had obviously absorbed somebody else's ideas. People aren't born that way. I wonder if children receive any guidance in school about how to treat disabled persons.

Why me?

Many times I've been told that I'm unlucky to have known a normal life because it allows me to make comparisons with my present life. Presumably, those who were born disabled are more content because "that's the way it's always been." There may be some truth in this. For many of us disabled through accident or disease that came later in life, comparison *is* inevitable.

In every facet of our life — work, family life, friendships and social interaction — things have changed. And, sad to say, some people who knew us as vital, energetic, articulate members of society tend to shy away from us as disabled persons. They're not uncaring or malicious but simply uncertain about how to treat us. Hello! We're still ourselves, which means we *do* get angry and frustrated and often feel sorry for ourselves. Of course we had all of those feelings before but we may have had an easier time concealing them.

No one suggests that handicapped people are perfect. I've heard from strangers that they've tried to ask questions or offer help to a disabled person, who promptly bit their head off. That's wrong, of course. Even if a disabled person is angry at life, he or she has no right to take it out on another person. So it works both ways. There needs to be more education — more acceptance — on both sides of the street.

In my own case, I had excellent training in anger management. Running a couple of restaurants meant having to deal as calmly as possible with the occasional irate customer or annoying employee. (Having four kids didn't hurt, either.) At the restaurant I learned to bite my tongue and sidestep potentially nasty confrontation. After keeping my cool through one of these incidents, however, I'd head for the bathroom and give the biffy a good swift kick or two. Not great for the toes but a dandy way to relieve the tension and regain a sense of perspective.

It's inevitable to be angry when you become disabled. In fact, I had a hard time accepting the fact that I was no longer "normal." Then you begin to see your life changing dramatically, your options diminishing, while everyone around you moves on with their lives. Like others in my predicament, I've faced the sense of hopelessness and despair that comes when you feel you're totally useless. Since kicking the toilet is no longer an option (I'd no doubt end up flat on my back on the floor), I've had to develop a new coping mechanism. It involves reminding myself that how I am is a fact, that I have to make the best of what I've got. It may not be much but over time you learn that it does no good to rave and rant and lose your temper. All you do is alienate the people around you and they'll start to shun you. If you want to keep friends and family in your life, it's essential to hold back on the anger and self-pity. Let them see that you're still you. Sure, we were often difficult before and we're still difficult sometimes. We're still the same people. In my case, I still smoke, I still take the odd drink, I still swear when the occasion demands it. My personality hasn't changed; only my body.

I still have two good friends — one in Calgary, one in Camrose. They've always known what I was like and they see that nothing has changed in that department. To them, my disability doesn't make any difference. I was Dianne then. I'm Dianne now. We've always been quite outspoken with each other and we still are. They can give me a hard time about the way I walk, for example, but I don't take it personally. The kindest thing anyone can do is to treat me as they always have. And if that means prodding me to change my ways or expecting me to occasionally laugh at myself, that's all the better. If I spill something when I'm visiting friends in Calgary, for example, they say, "Dianne, you made the mess you clean it up." That's great. They're treating me like a normal person.

On the other hand, I believe that the disabled person's reaction has a lot to do with shaping society's attitudes. If well-meaning people have a bad experience with someone who is disabled, it scares them off. They won't take a chance again and that's sad.

Help! It's the helping professions again!

Anyone who has been ill, in an accident or in need of medical assistance knows there are many dedicated professionals out there who relate well to their patients and do wonders to relieve their mental distress and physical pain.

I've recently learned, however, that not all members of the so-called helping professions have the knack of dealing well with disabled folks. Everyone, both able-bodied and disabled, has witnessed the stresses on today's health care system and, admittedly, dealing with a disabled person often requires extra time and attention. Perhaps talking to someone with a speech impairment simply takes too much time out of an already overburdened schedule.

In my own case, I can only believe that was the problem during one recent visit to the doctor. I had earlier visited his office because of one health problem but on this occasion I was there for an entirely different reason. When asked if I could see the doctor, the nurse said that wasn't possible and that she could do the follow-up on my earlier problem. The trouble was, I wasn't there for that reason, but the nurse simply wouldn't listen while I tried to explain why I needed to see the doctor. I know I talk funny, but that doesn't mean I've lost my ability to think. A "there, there" attitude hardly does the trick when you have a genuine health concern.

On another occasion I was told curtly to sit still and keep quiet. I had tried to enquire about a procedure the doctor was involved in. Obviously, not a smart move on my part.

I couldn't help contrasting these incidents — and others I've experienced or witnessed in recent months — with the excellent treatment I had always expected and received before I became disabled. I'm sure my medical needs are being looked after as they always were. I'm not so sure about the emotional needs. It's a disturbing thought but is it possible that some of the very people we trust and count on the most to help us cope with our disabilities are adding to our problems? Bedside manner and the sensitive treatment of patients is no doubt taught in medical schools and professional courses for caregivers. I'm wondering if there are courses on treating disabled folks who may have trouble moving about or have a hard time expressing their concerns? Disabled people have a lot on their plate without having to cope with additional barriers to the help they need.

Taking advantage

It's hard to believe, but every now and then being disabled can work to one's advantage. I freely admit that on occasion I've used my physical limitations to get what I want. When people see my awkward movements, for example, they tend to take over and do things for me. Sometimes it annoys me. Other times, I think, "oh, what the hell, let them go ahead and help. It's easier this way."

I've also been known to use my condition to elicit sympathy. This is a great ploy when you're trying to raise funds, for example. I've yet to meet anyone face to face who could look at my wheelchair and eyepatch and refuse to contribute to whatever fundraising effort I'm involved in.

My friend and I also learned the power of the disability factor during a visit to West Edmonton Mall. Wandering through the mall, chatting and window shopping for things we couldn't afford, we suddenly realized we would be late meeting her husband for lunch in the food court. The push was on to get down those marble hallways with the speed of light. But the crowds were huge and I wasn't exactly in sprinting mode. Then, to our amazement, we realized what was happening. As we pushed through the lineup, I began to notice that my cane and eyepatch were paying dividends. People might have been being kind and considerate. Or they might have feared they'd be mowed down by the approaching juggernaut as I wobbled along with my friend clutching on to my coattails. Whatever the reason, it was amazing to see the crowd open a path for us. It was the first time I had actually noticed the reaction of ordinary people to the disabled. Later, we compared it to the parting of the waves on the Red Sea. They say there's no situation so negative that you can't find something positive to latch on to!

The honour of working

It's unlikely any disabled Canadian will ever be left to starve without financial help of any kind. Programs such as AISH and the Canada Pension Plan have provided a financial lifeline for disabled persons. And clearly recent improvements to Alberta's AISH program are welcome, not only for the increased financial help but also for the opportunity to earn more supplemental income without penalty.

Still, I can't help wondering how many handicapped persons who might have been contributors to society have over the years been considered instead simply problems to be dealt with. Why should this be? Is it simply too much trouble to assess the potential of someone who doesn't fit into the "normal" world, then train that person to do useful work?

Hopefully society's attitudes are changing, but for far too many people with mental or physical shortcomings, the traditional answer was simply to warehouse them. I witnessed this myself, as someone close to me lived for many years in a home for the disabled, learning very little if anything about coping in society. Later, in a group home setting with almost one-to-one care and attention, she has learned to relate to others and to handle simple tasks. As part of a crowd in the institution, it's unlikely anyone expected much from her. Treated as a person and with love and patience in her new setting, she is learning to have some pride in herself and what she can do. She now has a job — and it makes a huge difference to her sense of worth. Her work may be a simple matter of filling the salt and pepper shakers — but her obvious pride in doing a job and doing it well is heart warming to see.

On one occasion I spoke to a lady who runs a coffee shop. She told me she had two employees, one of whom, a girl called Sara, was disabled. Based on her experience, she said, if she had to choose just one employee, it would be the disabled girl. Committed to pleasing an employer who was giving her a chance, Sara took enormous pride in her work. As evidence of this, her employer pointed to a fridge which shone like a mirror — proof of the importance Sara placed on a job that was truly her own.

I've heard countless stories like this over the years, leaving me to wonder if society in general shouldn't have higher expectations of those of us with handicaps. No one who hires a disabled person should expect a shoddy job. Perhaps it might take a little extra time to explain clearly what's needed. And it may require accepting some unorthodox ways of getting the job done. But if you're teaching someone to tie their shoelaces, does it really matter how they do it as long as the laces get tied? Normal folks tend to judge people by what they see. If they'd just dig down a bit, they might be surprised what they would find in a disabled person. This may take a while. Handicapped people tend not to trust people immediately. But in the long run, taking the time will surely be worth it. With a little patience, employers are likely to find their disabled employees are among their most loyal and reliable staff members.

Chapter - 6.

COMING TO TERMS WITH REALITY

Dianne wearing the famed "pirate patch" in 1993.

Anyone who has read this far is aware I have a burr under my blanket when it comes to disabled people. I've had it since I became handicapped. I know that unless something directly affects you, you don't pay that much attention. It's like trying to explain to a man what it's like to have a baby. I was no different. When we had the restaurants, I really couldn't have cared less if a person was purple, pink, using a cane or in a wheelchair. As long as they paid their bill of course. Was this a commendable lack of prejudice? The ability to see beyond the handicap to the person? Or was it simply a lack of time and empathy? I suspect I really never thought about what it would feel like to be disabled. When you're young, strong and busy, it's not a subject one is likely to dwell on.

I've had plenty of time to think about it since. And although I can only truly draw on my own experience, I feel I'm speaking for the many who, like myself, must face the reality of disability. No one can truly prepare you for the changes you will encounter as a newly disabled person. But, having been there, I feel qualified to offer a few insights.

Personal relationships: You need family and friends

Adapting to a disability — whether sudden or gradual in nature — creates a kind of Catch 22. You realize your energy and your customary sense of control and self-determination are disappearing — at the very time when you need all the strength you can muster to meet new challenges. In short, you need help and, for most of us, having to ask for help can diminish self confidence and the will to carry on.

Newly dependent on family and friends, we tend to seesaw between fighting for our independence and increasingly looking for assistance in everything from household tasks to transportation. Fear, despair, uncertainty and anger become part of our daily lives. In my own case, lack of mobility and communication problems, both of which tend to isolate me, have been particularly frustrating. There was a time when those who know me best pointed out that I would argue with God Himself, if I felt strongly enough about an issue. For much of my life, I was accustomed to counseling and advising others. Wasn't I the one who had most of the answers? Learning to keep my opinions to myself has been a struggle.

If I had a single bit of advice for the newly disabled, it would be to remember that family and friends are simply people. They have their own problems and your misfortune doesn't automatically make saints of those around you. While you soon learn who you can depend on, you can't expect your near and dear to always put your needs first and give you special treatment. For myself, I've discovered that, rather than coddling, encouragement and practical assistance when it's really needed are the keys to helping me live a near-normal life.

Relationships with family are one thing; encounters with strangers another. Perhaps some of my speech problems are related to constantly biting my tongue to keep from exploding when strangers treat me as a second — no, third or fourth — class citizen. I recall one incident where a home care worker and I were in a store. I wasn't in a great mood to begin with; the lineups at the tills seemed endless; and everyone was getting frustrated. Another shopper complained aloud about the fact my wheelchair was holding up the line. He picked the wrong day. I quietly invited him to take a long walk on a short pier. I'll never forget the look on his face. He didn't say a word but it was obvious what he was thinking: "Eeeek, it talks!" If I hadn't been biting my tongue at the time, I might have asked him how long it was since he'd taken a bath.

Why do some people think it's okay to be rude to anyone with a visible handicap? Although I've known long-term disabled folks who say they're accustomed to put downs, this lack of respect can come as a devastating shock to the newly disabled. As so-called normal people, we rarely, if ever, received such treatment. Does our appearance invite insults? Or, in the minds of unthinking passers by, does our loss of mobility equate to a loss of intelligence and normal human feelings? Once, when I was shopping with a nurse/companion, she met a friend who quickly dismissed me with a few condescending remarks that made me feel like a four-year-old. My companion was horrified. She asked if people always treated me that way? When I confirmed that it happened more often than not, she couldn't believe it. Like me, she wondered if many folks simply don't know any better? If that's the case, it's another reason to consider an aggressive program of public education about disabled persons.

Finances: What will I do without a job?

Disabled persons are unlikely to wind up millionaires. That's not to say it hasn't happened. But, for the most part, we recognize that being disabled equates to living modestly, probably at or below the poverty line. Even if we have marketable skills or can be trained to earn some independent income, most of us are realistic enough to know that prosperity or even middle income status are pretty well out for us. Even so, financial concerns often take a back seat to other, more pressing, issues such as transportation, education, housing, prejudice, mobility and access.

In fact, governments apparently spend millions on us disabled folks and no one can deny that the cheques come in on schedule. Granted, we need more money if we're to enjoy anything in the way of perks. And clearly more help, more encouragement and more opportunities are needed for those who could be gainfully employed. On the other hand, the ability to respond quickly and efficiently with financial support — adequate or not — is one thing government seems to have got right. In my own case, social agencies responded when I was left to cope with both my growing disability and a growing family. Later, when I was older and increasingly disabled, I began depending on CPP, AISH, and Aids to Daily Living. Perhaps it's simpler to write a cheque than to wade through the complexities of public education and changes in society's perceptions and attitudes toward disabled persons. Besides, in my present situation, I have so little opportunity for shopping, recreation or other extracurricular activities, I can make a little money go a long way.

I believe an even bigger question is: Why should I be without a job? It may be getting too late for me, but more and more people in my situation are saying: "I'm physically disabled, not brain dead. I have intelligence, aptitudes, the ability to learn and to contribute. A monthly cheque is nice but, for most of us, a chance to earn both a living and some respect in society would be even nicer." It won't be easy. Government funding bodies, policy-makers, educators, social agencies and employers will all have to be involved.

Society in general will have to want change, will have to realize that a whole generation is being lost to society, and will have to understand that a huge resource is being wasted. In Alberta, particularly, where workplace skills are at a premium, tapping into the potential of thousands of disabled people would be good for the province, good for society and a huge boost to the well-being and self-confidence of so many people.

Where will I live?

It doesn't take a degree in economics to figure out that income and housing are closely linked. For disabled persons, this link can lead to a list of pretty dismal options. Affordable housing is virtually non-existent in many communities. Publicly-owned institutions for the severely disabled may take up some of the slack. Bunking in with family members is the answer for some. Many disabled folks stretch a modest income by sharing a home with others on disability pensions. None of these options is ideal; all have a devastating impact on any effort at independence.

My own search for a place to live that was affordable and gave me some independence went on for years, finally ending in Lloydminster — on the Saskatchewan side of the border. I found that, there, the percentage of income required for government subsidized housing was 25% compared to 30% on the Alberta side. That sounded good to me. Having been born and brought up in Saskatchewan, I had come full circle. I had also come to realize that in my '40s and '50s — the time when most moderately successful people are renovating their homes or "moving on up" in the housing market — I would require government help to stay in even the most modest apartment. Facing up to reality doesn't always come easy.

After moving to Lloydminster, I was soon involved in several initiatives related to improving the lot of persons with disabilities. And, as I'll explain in another chapter, much of my effort centered around the need for a fresh look at the housing needs of low-income folks, both disabled and non-disabled.

Getting there isn't always 'half the fun!'

Issues surrounding transportation, mobility and access loom large in the life of those who, because of physical or mental impairment, can't simply get in the car and go. For those of us who have driven for decades, giving up a driver's license can be the ultimate insult to our lives. Where does that leave us? Many of us can't use public transit (although some jurisdictions such as Grande Prairie deserve kudos for ensuring disabled folks get free public transportation). DATS and Handibus systems are a wonderful idea but these services are generally limited and not available in many smaller communities. When it comes to long distance transport, airlines that require disabled people to fly with an attendant often expect payment for the extra seat — a problem I'm happy to say is now being addressed by one advocacy group for the disabled. And, although it's hard to believe, some railway cars have aisles too narrow to accommodate wheelchairs. Again, railway officials are apparently listening and changes are under way.

"Getting there" is one of the major barriers we face. Despite genuine progress in terms of access for the handicapped, disabled folks in many areas are virtual prisoners in their own homes. Many excellent, well intentioned programs that provide training, education or recreation for the disabled aren't available to the very people they are designed to help. Is it possible that some of the money funneled into programs for the disabled could be spent instead on paying attendants who could work with one or more disabled "clients," acting as chauffeurs and assistants to ensure they have access to these resources? Perhaps some disabled — but mobile — folks could actually fill these slots, producing a double benefit: mobility for otherwise homebound disabled persons and financial gain for others.

There is no question that governments and charitable agencies genuinely try to improve life for the disabled. Add a bit of creative thinking, and the results could be overwhelmingly positive.

Most jurisdictions have made great strides in recent years in providing wheelchair access. Still, send any wheelchair-bound person on a tour of the town and he or she will almost certainly say the guidelines appear to be inconsistent at best — and ignored at worst. Gently sloping sidewalks can suddenly give way to steep drops. Getting down may be possible but forget negotiating such obstacles on the way up.

Those of us who depend on our wheels rather than our legs to get around, soon learn to avoid businesses that make only token efforts to accommodate this large segment of the population. For example, I've talked to one lady who was able to get her wheelchair into a public washroom, only to find the doors on the cubicles were too narrow to allow wheelchair access. Another encountered trouble getting into a washroom because of a curved wall leading up to the door — a charming architectural detail perhaps but a genuine pain when nature calls. I have personally encountered access problems at one of Canada's leading coffee houses. By the time I and other wheelchair types managed the circuitous route to the entrance, we were ready to give it up and go home. Does anyone in a wheelchair test these routes? What a great opportunity for a focus group with the right credentials!

Time to smarten up!

For most so-called normal people, education begins with the basics of reading, writing and arithmetic. For disabled folks, the very first lesson should focus on learning to value oneself. I'm convinced that low self-esteem is one trait all disabled persons share. Those of us who can recall how we judged ourselves as normal people may have a better chance of maintaining a sense of self-worth. But for the thousands who don't have that touchstone, there's the inevitable sense of being second class, unworthy of the respect and consideration most of the world takes for granted. As one friend put it, it's time to get rid of those footprints on our faces.

Can self-confidence be taught? In the right environment with the right teachers and role models, I'm convinced it can be. More one-on-one or small group contact would be a great start. Anyone in the teaching profession will tell you there's extra work involved when students are physically, mentally or emotionally challenged. However, most believe that extra work is worth it. Given the right tools, they're ready to make the effort. Improved access to education, training and recreation programs and resources would be another step forward. Millions of dollars are being funneled into programs that, all too often, never reach the people who most need the help. They can't cope with the transportation problems. Get us there and watch us blossom!

Education is a two-way street. Society in general could benefit from new attitudes toward the disabled. Although most North Americans tend to think of themselves as part of a kind and caring society, folks who come surrounded by wheelchairs and other paraphernalia quickly discover discrimination in virtually every field that impacts their lives. It may not be deliberate. Thoughtlessness, ignorance and impatience are all part of the picture. A good, strong public relations campaign would be a good start. Society in general can be taught to look beyond the disability to see the person. I'm convinced a little creative thinking in this regard could result in initiatives that would be just as valuable to a disabled person as some of costly support programs now funded by government.

Chapter - 7

LIVING AND LEARNING TOGETHER

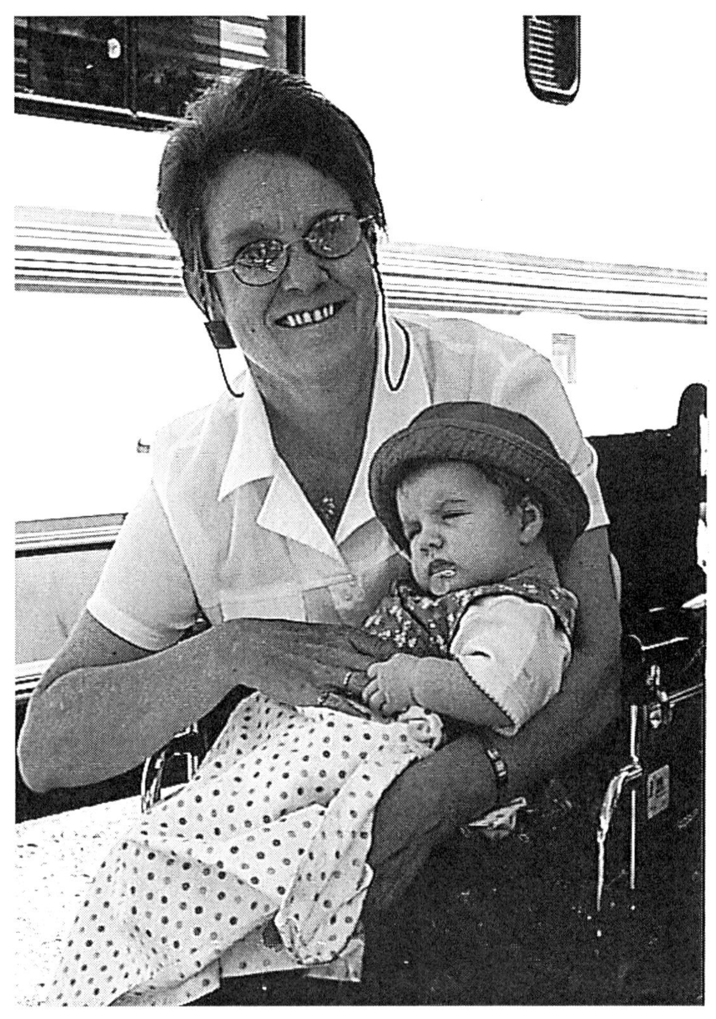

Grandma Dianne in 1999.

I remember somebody once saying that he never truly disliked anyone he really got to know. It's a matter of getting over those first impressions, looking beyond the myths, destroying the stereotypes — to genuinely see the person behind them. Of course this is easier said than done but in the case of the handicapped and mainstream communities, surely any effort toward mutual learning and understanding would be worthwhile.

This was the thinking behind a group I helped establish and chaired in Lloydminster during the late 1990s. We called it the Lloydminster Special Needs Housing Group.

We were promoting low-income housing that would welcome both the handicapped and ordinary people. We envisioned a building equipped with an elevator so that disabled folks using a wheelchair or walker wouldn't be forced to live solely on the main floor. Disabled persons would be given priority but everyone would be welcome to apply. Through interaction, both sides would surely discover some surprising things about each other. It wouldn't happen overnight but, in our view, it would be a sound beginning.

Among strong supporters of our cause was the Lloydminster Association for Community Living (LACL), an organization that provided a wide variety of information and recreational resources to the community. We were also able to get some influential government people involved — people in a position to get something done. Everyone thought it was a great housing concept, but getting money was something else again. We soon learned that, since Lloydminster straddles the border between two provinces, it's hard to get things done. Alberta and Saskatchewan often seemed like two kids playing in the sand. Each tries to keep the other out of the sandbox. In our case, we were proposing a housing complex that would have been open to people from both the Saskatchewan and Alberta sides of the city.

At the time, even those handicapped people who were perfectly capable of living independently, were unable to find affordable housing on their small CPP or AISH incomes. We weren't alone in realizing this. On the Alberta side, for example, a 1993 report outlining response to recommendations of the Premier's Council on the Status of Persons with Disabilities underscored this point. It read, "A shortage of accessible and affordable housing for persons with disabilities still exists....There is progress but it is somewhat slow moving." In Lloydminster, we quietly said "Amen" to this and went to work on our own project.

At one point we had found a site close to a shopping centre with all services such as a grocery store and bank nearby. We had a contractor willing to build and it looked like our project would go ahead. The proposal had gone through two readings at City Hall and we were confident our goals would be accomplished. Sadly, the proposal was defeated on third reading. It turned out there were a few complaints. One man felt a building on the proposed site would block the sun from his garden. Perhaps he could have moved his garden to the other side of his lot? Also residents in the area worried about increased traffic flow. The plan never did get off the ground although a man from Social Services later told me that, after the next civic election, it would have had a much better chance of success. Unfortunately I left Lloydminster soon after that so I'm not aware what has happened.

If my experience with the special needs housing group taught me anything, it is that disabled folks can take an active role in seeking improvements to services and opportunities available to them. We can be proactive. Along the way I have served on the board of the Lloydminster Handivan Society, belonged to the Lloydminster and Area Brain Injury Society and was active with the Lloydminster Association for Community Living, Family Support Network. Earlier, in Camrose, I served on the Board of Directors of the National Access Awareness Week. With regard to the latter, I've always thought a sure sign of success would be when there is no longer a need for an "awareness" week — when society has developed a true understanding of the needs of disabled persons and has learned to view us, first and foremost, as people. It's a simple concept — and what a positive step in ensuring that those with special needs have equal opportunities to experience life and make a contribution to society.

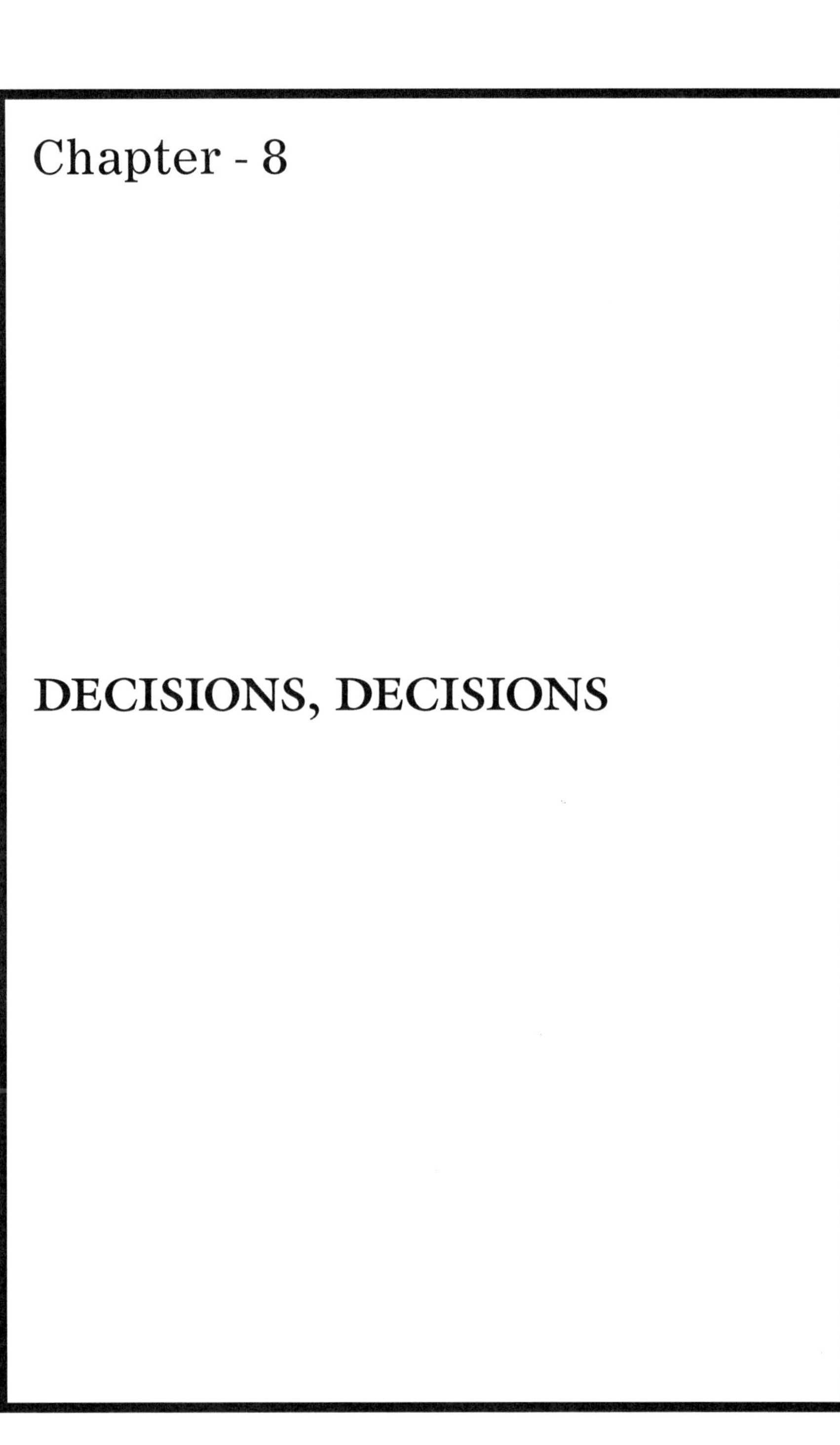

Chapter - 8

DECISIONS, DECISIONS

It occurs to me that everything I have said so far boils down to one thing: the inability of disabled persons to make their own decisions. So much of our life is governed by others' decisions — decisions made by family members, guardians, government policy wonks, the medical community and social and charitable agencies. I assume all act with our best interests in mind. Obviously no one is out to "get us" because of some shortcoming in our physical or mental state. And, to be fair, sometimes our own infirmities make the decisions for us.

However objectively we look at it, most of us agree that the inability to decide for ourselves can be one of the most frustrating aspects of our disability. Where we go depends on someone else's decisions about transportation and access. When we go is linked to the decisions of attendants or caregivers who give us their time and attention. Where we live is often dictated by government decision-makers who fund support programs for the disabled. Sadly, without the ability to make our own choices, we tend to feel that we are being treated as things rather than people.

What can be done to change the situation? Again, the first step is to realize we are people, *not* simply disabled people. Behind our canes and wheelchairs and walkers and hearing aids and seeing eye dogs and mechanical lifts, we are people — human beings with all of the hopes and desires of people everywhere. Perhaps we can't climb mountains or compete in marathons. Lots of so-called normal people aren't great at those activities either. What, for the most part, we *can* do however, is have some input into decisions that affect our lives.

Most disabled folks I've met are pretty reasonable. We're not likely to demand the unattainable. Admittedly, our lives are cumbersome. It's tough to be spontaneous when you're tied to a wheelchair or an oxygen bottle. Still, our input should count for something. Few of us, if any, expect miracles to change our situation. But, how great it would be to be part of the decision-making process. A few minutes spent in discussion, a brief look at the pros and cons, a chance to express our views and preferences would do much to counter the feelings of helplessness that tend to engulf us. I suspect that more often than not we'd come to the same conclusion as those who make decisions for us. But we'd have been part of the process — and that would make all the difference.

Much of what I have written is based on personal experience although my contacts with disabled people in all walks of life tell me that many others share my thoughts and feelings. Of course we're frustrated. We're often angered by situations that seem incredibly unfair. But we're much more than simply a problem to be dealt with. Collectively we're a human resource of major proportions. Let's hope that future generations don't look back on the 21st century and realize that here was a resource that was never developed. All of us — disabled folks, caregivers, educators, governments, communities, society at large —have the ability to capitalize on what we have. It will take time, patience, understanding and the will to make a change. Society has already made genuine progress in smoothing the way for disabled persons. But much more needs to be done. I'm convinced that, in Canada, we have everything we need to make it happen.

Chapter - 9

WHERE'S DIANNE? HERE SHE IS!

Behind the disability Dianne is still here, engaged in her trademark talking, nagging, cajoling, persuading. The voice may not be as clear as it once was, but the will to be heard remains as strong as ever. Happily, there's no need to counsel revolution. The goal is not to turn the system upside down, merely to encourage a few modest, common sense changes that could pay huge dividends for both disabled folks and society as a whole.

If these changes are so simple and common sense, why haven't they occurred long before this? Earlier I likened today's attitudes toward the disabled to society's attitude toward the Holocaust. Good and decent people the world over were apparently unaware of what was happening to many of their fellow human beings. Was it simply a case of "out of sight, out of mind?" Was the truth ignored out of indifference and apathy? Is it possible that the same attitude prevails today — not toward victims of concentration camps, but to those who are ignored, overlooked, sidelined simply because they don't fit society's definition of "normal?"

In the 21st century are we destined to repeat — admittedly on a different level — that great tragedy of the 20th century? Remaining blind to the lost potential of tens of thousands of North Americans, simply because the problems seem insurmountable, suggest that's just what's happening. This time the prejudice has nothing to do with race or religion. It simply has to do with disability. An entire generation of disabled persons — those who suffer from physical, mental or emotional impairment — is being ignored. Not with evil intent. Simply through indifference. Whatever the reason, thousands are left without any meaningful education, encouragement or support to participate in society. Behind closed doors, they simply sit and wait.

Nothing I've written to date is new or particularly innovative. The problems I've addressed are not unique to me. All disabled folks I know share them. They simply reflect the way things are. If, like me, you question *why* this is the way things are, you might want to consider the following suggestions.

Checklist for change

1. Let's start by uncoupling the worlds "disabled" and "person." When we meet new people, we don't automatically describe them as old, young, pleasant, cranky, fat, thin etc. Think "people" first. The adjectives can come later. Remember, you're meeting an individual, not a disability.

2. A strong public education program is needed to change society's perceptions of those with disabilities. It's time people of *all* abilities are seen as an asset to be nourished rather than a liability to be dealt with, or worse, ignored. Viewed simply as a problem, millions of Canadians are currently barred from active participation in the community. In the midst of today's labour shortages, this huge potential resource can no longer be overlooked.

3. Education should be top of the list in efforts to improve the quality of life for those with physical, mental or emotional disabilities. For the disabled, the focus must first be on nurturing self-esteem and a sense of self-worth. For society at large, the goal should be improved awareness that everyone, regardless of mental or physical limitations, has value to the community, and deserves respect and inclusion in society. It's a lesson that must be taught early in life and continually reinforced.

4. For many persons with disabilities, lack of mobility keeps them from taking advantage of the very programs designed to improve their situation. Some of the billions of dollars spent annually on support programs for the disabled community could be better spent paying for more one-on-one assistance, including help with transportation. Solving the transportation problem would remove a huge barrier to training, recreation and employment for thousands of disabled people.

5. Innovative housing schemes that bring together people with disabilities and other low-income people would be mutually beneficial, encouraging education, awareness and acceptance among disabled and able-bodied residents. Some initiatives of this kind have been launched; many more are needed.

6. Some medical staff and others in the helping professions would benefit from refresher courses in the treatment of persons with disabilities. Awkward movements and difficulty in speaking or hearing do not indicate lack of intelligence or lack of feelings. Those with mental or physical impairments deserve to be treated with the kind of dignity and respect so-called normal patients receive.

7. Employment opportunities for disabled people need to be increased. Potential employers should be made aware that any extra time and effort required for training will pay off in terms of loyal, positive, dependable employees. Government-sponsored employment programs for the disabled, such as "Chrysalis," are a step in the right direction.

8. Policy-makers at all levels should revisit the issue of access for people using walkers or wheelchairs. Great strides have been made but jurisdictions and businesses don't always adhere to the guidelines, creating some nasty surprises for disabled users of buildings, roads and sidewalks.

9. Social agencies and caregivers must be encouraged to include the disabled person in the decision-making process. We accept that our disabilities often limit our choices, but common courtesy suggests we should have some input into decisions that affect our lives.

10. Authorities must adopt a zero-tolerance attitude toward any form of bullying or harassment of persons with physical or developmental limitations. Disabled persons don't ask for pity or preferential treatment. They do expect and deserve to be treated with civility and respect.

Chapter - 10

A FINAL THOUGHT

In the two years since I began writing this book, a lot has changed. As I mentioned, one particularly severe seizure in 2004 took its toll and, rather than using a walker, I now depend exclusively on a wheelchair. On the plus side, I receive excellent care and consideration from Chateau Sturgeon staff and various therapists are helping me make the best use of whatever strength and mobility remains.

On a personal note, I have much to be thankful for. My four children all now live within a short distance of my current home so help is at hand if I need it. I'm told my speech is gradually improving. Either my audience is catching on to my lingo — or I've learned to talk a bit more slowly. Weekly sessions with a speech therapist are helping. Also, I've noticed that when I make out a cheque, my signature actually appears on the line instead of straggling all over the place — proof that the strengthening exercises are paying off. Even small signs of improvement are encouraging.

I take some comfort as well in the fact that more and more individuals and advocacy groups are speaking out about disability issues. For example, the CNIB has just reported that only 25% of Canada's blind or visually impaired citizens of working age have employment — a shocking statistic that apparently hasn't budged in several decades. What a huge pool of talent and energy is being wasted as thousands of potentially productive Canadians are sidelined by disability. Why is this the case in one of the most economically advanced and enlightened countries in the world? One has to wonder if society is listening. Let's hope that decades from now, no one will say: "We didn't know what was happening."

Postscript

Since writing this book, I have witnessed some progress in areas which have been of particular concern to myself and others. For example, a public education program was recently launched by the government to encourage employment of disabled persons. Much more needs to be done, of course, but I applaud this step in the right direction — a sign that those who can make things happen are indeed beginning to listen!

ISBN 142513168-9

9 781425 131685